The Path
of the Mothers

The Path
of the Mothers

Biblical Women:
Poetry and Inspiration for
Growth and Transformation

Carol Rose

Illustrations by
Lu-Ann Lynde

Albion
Andalus
Boulder, Colorado
2015

"The old shall be renewed,
and the new shall be made holy."
— Rabbi Avraham Yitzhak Kook

Albion-Andalus Inc.
P. O. Box 19852
Boulder, CO 80308
www.albionandalus.com

Design and composition by Albion-Andalus Inc.

Cover design by Sari Wisenthal-Shore.

Cover image of the oil painting, "Miriam the Prophetess" by Anselm
Feuerbach.

Author photo by Larry Flynn.

Manufactured in the United States of America

ISBN-13: 978-0692409138 (Albion-Andalus Books)
ISBN-10: 0692409130

This book is dedicated to all who
bring light to the journey ...
my teachers, my children,
my students, my friends.

Contents

Acknowledgments

THANKS TO NETANEL MILES-YÉPEZ for your gentle invitation to have the images become part of the lovely spiritual library that you continue to produce, and to Jennifer Phares Miles for typing out the poems and scanning the images. I'd also like to thank Rev. Paul Campbell and my students at the Faculty of Theology at the University of Winnipeg. Your insight, guidance and feed back have graced this project from the beginning! Special thanks to Sr. Mary Coswin and the folks at St. Benedict's educational center for hosting "Walking the Mother Path" and "Listening to Our Inner Prophetesses" workshops. I am grateful to my 'sisters of light' (the members of Achyot Or) who have experimented with this work at several of our unforgettable retreats. Thanks, to Dr. Ulla Ryum for bringing me to Denmark, and to the communities in Canada, the United States and Israel who walked The Mother Path with me. Thanks to the Manitoba Arts Council and the Winnipeg Arts Council for their support and travel grants. And, as always, to Neal who has been my most wonderful coach and advisor. Thank you to my children for joining us in midrash making … and for teaching us so much.

— C.R.

Preface

I WOULD LIKE TO EXPRESS my heart-and-soul-felt gratitude to Rabbi Zalman Schachter Shalomi, z"l, who encouraged me to work on what he called "a women's path through Torah" sometime in 1984 or 1985.

Although the original "Walking the Mother Path" cards that I created did not manifest as the 32 paths he envisioned as a form of women's Kabbalah, the images and poems were certainly "a received" women's tradition, and it is this received tradition that we now hope to bring to our readers. Although the work first appeared as a set of cards called "Walking The Mother Path," used in workshops, retreats and educational settings throughout the United States, Canada, Denmark, and Israel, I have long felt the need to bring them together in book form, as well.

The truth is that I had wanted to create this work in honor of our daughter, Adira Tiferet Nesya, who was about to enter our family. Our four sons were already intimately familiar with biblical heroes, and I wanted Adira to have similar opportunities to engage with the women in our sacred tradition. What I discovered as I studied and read was that much of what we knew about biblical women was sketchy, or possibly one dimensional, whether the stories came directly from the Bible or from the various commentaries offered by our Rabbis. These sacred stories (about women) were all being told and analyzed by men … by those who did not share the same life-experiences and challenges that women faced. I saw our task as trying to embody the women—trying to live in their skin—and create more expansive and vivid images of their lives. I began imagining biblical women; sensing what their lives were like from a woman-centered perspective. I shone the spotlight on each of the situations they faced. They became central to their own story, not just adjuncts to the actions of the men in the narrative. I imagined them in my waking life, and in my dreams. They were my familiars, my constant companions.

I tried to read whatever I could by women theologians from various faith communities. I attended women's workshops in Canada and the United States (thanks Carol Stewart for having me create a ritual for the four biblical mothers: Sarah, Rebekah, Rachel and Leah, which later became the seed from which this project continued to grow). I also talked to everyone I knew about our matriarchs, gathering oral as well as written midrashim. Then I put out a call for an artist.

I would like to honor artist/illustrator Lu-Ann Lynde for the holy way in which we were able to work together. When we met, Lu-Ann told me she'd received two gifts from her grandmother. One was a Bible that she hoped to use in our weekly study sessions. While Lu-Ann did use her grandmother's Bible (for study and meditation at home), when we worked together, we used fifteen or more Hebrew Bibles and various commentaries and dissected each story that contained even a hint of the life of a biblical women.

We studied, discussed, argued, and sometimes agreed upon the powerful archetypes that we were encountering. At the end of our session, Lu-Ann would cast the I Ching (a tool from her own spiritual practice) and we would sit with the reading, quietly reflecting on its teaching before returning to our separate lives. When the week was up, we would return with a sketch and a midrashic poem about the individual we had studied (and lived with) for that week. If we felt that there was a "match," we'd sit in silence and give thanks for the divine gift that we had received, and then we'd move on to investigate the next woman.

Frequently we felt that more than one image was necessary to represent a particular matriarch (Sarah, Rebekah, Rachel, Leah, Miriam, and Ruth). Sometimes we had questions that we couldn't resolve in dialogue, and we'd bring those to our Rosh Chodesh or women's groups, or sometimes we'd discuss them with friends (thanks Elana Schachter, Joan Turner, Elinor Johns, Kate Bitney, and R' Mimi Feigelson). In the case of Huldah, I recall being on two phone calls (simultaneously) checking with friends about an obscure Rashi commentary (thanks Lori Grysman and Harry Lakser).

Throughout the process we were committed to learning as much as we could, and then filtering what we learned through our own experiences. We called this being "transparent to the inside." We hoped to produce sketches and poems that would evoke further investigations of this type.

For more than 20 years I studied Imagery with my

beloved teacher, Madame Colette Aboulker-Muscat, in Jerusalem. During one of my classes with her I spoke about the project. Colette asked me to imagine the format and, quite spontaneously, I said, "I see an egg." Colette was delighted. "Your words and illustrations will be new seeds for women (and men) to contemplate." When I returned to Winnipeg, I mentioned the idea of producing egg-shaped cards to use as meditation and/or educational tools. Suddenly Lu-Ann grew very still. Then she asked, "Remember when we first met ... I told you that I had received two things from my grandmother?" I said that I indeed remembered. Then she continued, "Well, the other item that my grandmother left for me was an oval china frame, or a template. Now I know why ... I'll use it to center my drawings and your poems." If we needed any further validation that this project was being directed from above, this was it! For more than twenty years the images have appeared in the oval outline provided by Lu- Ann's grandmother's template.

Now The Path of the Mothers has found its way into your lives, dear reader. It is our hope that you will continue reading, commenting, questioning, and discovering new layers of meanings as you choose an image and reflect upon her. Glance at her, read the midrashic poem. Ask yourself, "Why have I chosen this particular matriarch? How does her life reflect realities that I am facing, or will face?" The questions are on-going, and I hope that our holy foremothers will become helpful companions to you on your journey toward greater self-understanding and mastery.

— Carol Rose, St. Louis, Missouri

Introduction

In 1985, I DESIGNED a set of cards with artist Lu-Ann Lynde called, "Walking the Motherpath." The cards were our attempt at midrash or interpretation of the lives of biblical women. Each oval-shaped card presented a sketch of one of the matriarchs accompanied by a poetic interpretation. There were also one word qualities (or characteristics) assigned to each of the women in the deck.

My hope was that the cards would serve as "mirrors of identity" or doorways into a greater sense of personal awareness, and that women and men could use the cards to unravel the stories of our ancient mothers in order to gain greater insight into our own life processes as well.

In creating the deck, our research included text study, an exploration of existing midrashim (interpretations), and our own dreams and imaginings. In some cases we used the interpretations gathered from our respective women's and Rosh Chodesh groups (as well as testing the project at Achyot Or retreats).

What we were trying to do (like Marion Zimmer Bradley's The Mists of Avalon) was to shift the emphasis of an entire body of history so that it included the experiences of women. Our task was complicated because we were trying to do this with so-called sacred text, with text respected for its continuity. And we were trying to do this as "insiders," as those who felt directed and commanded by the wisdom of the past.

Over the years, the cards have been used by individuals in many faith communities. They have become a vehicle for making the lives of our foremothers accessible. Individuals have used them in study groups as educational materials, and alone as meditative tools. Because our original intent was to "remain true" to an internal vision, we produced them as they came to us, sketch-like and technically imperfect. They were meant to evoke responses from those who interacted with them. They can be used at home or in small groups. One can open the book and turn to an image before prayer, or as part of a Friday night candle lighting ritual, or in conversation at the dinner table.

I have also used the cards in various workshops called "Walking the Motherpath" and "Listening to Our Inner Prophetesses." As a part of the workshop, an image was chosen randomly and served as a guide for directing seekers inward to the Source of Wisdom. These workshops were laboratories in which biblical women's stories could be re-imagined experientially. It is my hope that the book will provide opportunities for this same kind of exploration, opportunities for increasing our "image pool," and for expanding our understanding of the lives our matriarchs, from a woman-centered perspective. I believe the book is an effort toward Tikkun Olam, healing a previously unbalanced presentation of women in biblical narrative by inviting right brain thinking or imagination into the process.

The Path of the Mothers provides an opportunity to engage with stories housed in women's souls. It is my hope that the illustrations and midrashic poems evoke an awareness of the presence of the Shekinah (the Divine Feminine) in her many nuanced forms.

The Path
of the Mothers

SHEKINAH

Heart's hoary EYELID
Under whose covering
Crystal tears soften
Dreams, enabling
Vision's renewal.
Protecting lace CLOUD
Dancing o'er tentplace
Rays pirouetting
Through foggy vapors
Casting new light.
Gazellelike PRESENCE
Deepening the journey
With silvery imprints,
Carving a new road
Along steep path.

KNOWLEDGE

©1988. L·LYNDE
C·ROSE

EVE

EVE

In its likeness
The "All in One" formed
Earthcreature undifferentiated
Until the dream
In the midst of the garden
Where the four streams divide
There the Tree of the Knowledge
Of Opposites yields its fruit
And your nakedness Eve,
Becomes known, as the other half
Tastes, sees itself,
And empties of all projections
Then the invisable comes
Visable — the seperatenss
Yet oneness of all.

The Path of the Mothers

PROPHECY

© 1987 L·LYNDE
C·ROSE

SARAH

SARAH

You left known for unknown
Wanderer, princess,
Nuturing women teacher.
You shared the vision,
You hid, you laughed.
Clearsighted prophetess,
You revealed painful truths.
Catalyst, you made distinctions
And caused others to see.
You chose, with authority,
Birthed and died without models.
You dared to live
With SHEKINAH as friend.
You brought light to the tent
And you sustained it.

CATALYST

SARAH

REBEKAH

Born at the moment of change,
The AKADAH and Sarah's death,
You understood sacrifice;
One in place of the other.
At first you entered Sarah's tent
Closed, veiled virgin bride
Opening wider, wider, wider
To conceive, conceive it all.
Opposing energies wrestling
In your womb. You fought,
You heard GOD'S voice
And lived the promise,
The destiny of warriors and dreamers.

CHANGE

REBEKAH

CONFLICT

REBEKAH

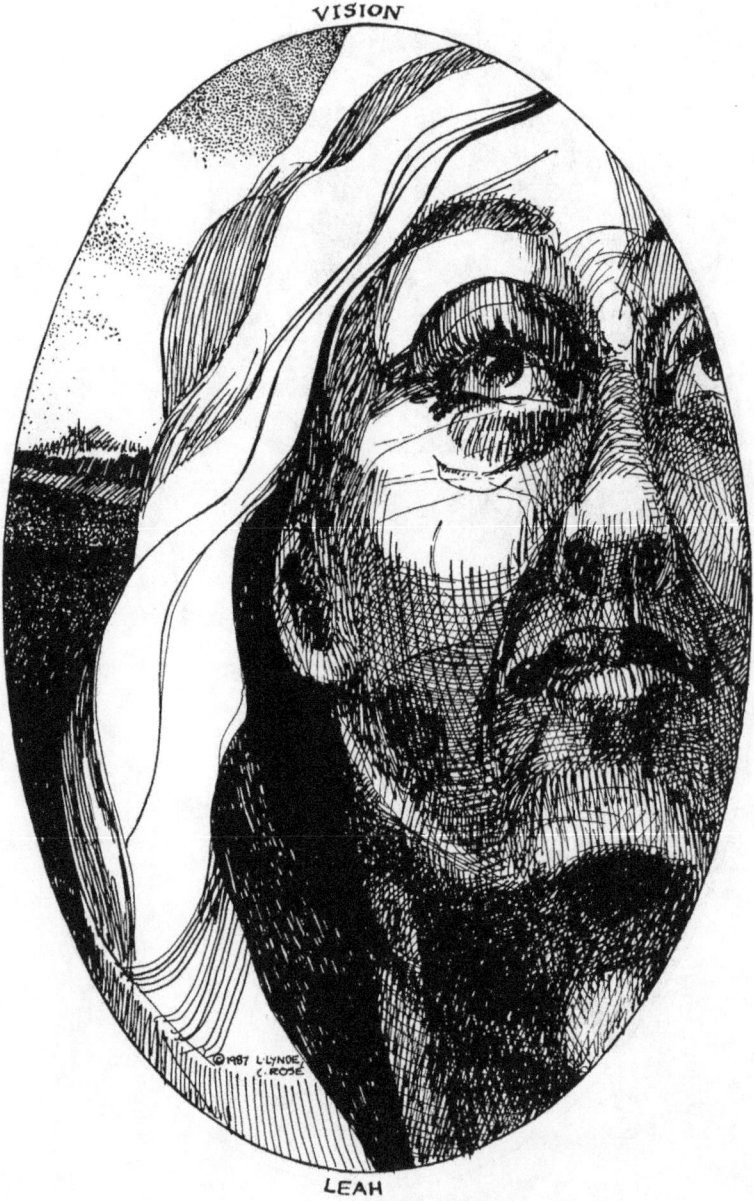

VISION

LEAH

LEAH

From Rebekah's house you learn
To change reality,
Order the world, in GOD'S name.
You claim your place
And pay dearly, Divine Ram.
Over and over again, mother,
You offer up your womb.
Sister of compassion
Trading mandrakes for love,
Wanting only your due.
Your tears purify vision,
You gaze with eyes of tenderness.

COMPASSION

LEAH

©1987 L·LYNDE,
C·ROSE

SACRIFICE

©1987 L·LYNDE,
C·ROSE

LEAH

FOCUS

©1987 L·LYNDE
C·ROSE

RACHEL

RACHEL

You drew his love at the well,
Generously bringing it to Leah
Under SHEKINAH'S canopy;
A union of mystery.
Like Jacob you wrestled
and sacrificed for blessing.
You birthed the future
Dying on the way, like Moses,
You struck the rock
And forced the waters;
Mingling waters flowing
With tears — ours/yours.
Your eternal cry urges
And bids us return, Mother.

GENEROSITY

©1987 L·LYNDE,
C·ROSE

RACHEL

RESOLUTION

©1987 L·LYNDE, C·ROSE

TAMAR

TAMAR

Sitting at the crossroads
You remove widow's garb
And veil yourself for him.
Covering eyes of ordinary sight
You invite love unavailable
And stretch beyond limits.
Your womb swells with promise,
The paradox resolves
In birth of redeemers and kings.

VULNERABILITY

©1988 L·LYNDE C·ROSE

DINAH

DINAH

Barefoot you come from tentbreast folds
Drawn by bouquets of warm winds
Caressing your legs, raising your skirts,
Urging flowers to spill their secret fragrances.
Your movement is open, vulnerable, light,
Touching all things to life with your step
Until lust rages unbalanced, and you fall,
Crying the cry that echoes eternally
In our hearts.

ABUNDANCE

©1987 L. LYNDE, C. ROSE

MIRIAM

MIRIAM

Assertive sister/child
Abundantly clear, strong.
Your prophecy is heard,
Men and women reunite
And birth freedom.
You quench their thirst,
Stepping over boundaries,
Advising, leading, dancing
The dance of celebration.

INTERCESSION

© 1988. L. LYNDE, C. ROSE.

TZIPPORAH

TZIPPORAH

Tzipporah darkened wife
Hosting desert dreamer.
Priestess offering water/blood
Appeasing thirst/anger.
Hands forever red,
Uprooting children, bloody
Wanderer — always on the
Outside — interceding —
Reminder of the stranger's
Strength.

CHALLENGE

TZELOPHCHAD'S DAUGHTERS

©1988·L·LYNDE, C·ROSE

Tzelophchad's Daughters

Belief in the land
And your rights therein,
Send princes and prophets
To meeting place within
The Tent where decisions
Divienly rendered
Challenge inheritance
Based solely on gender.
More equitable laws
Which grant each their share
End a tradition
Restricted by fear.

TRANSFORMATION

©1988 L·LYNDE C·ROSE

RAHAV

Rahav

Welcoming woman
Protecting and hiding
Invaders transforming
Beneath womb of flax.
Changing potential
Destruction to freedom
The cord of redemption
Held firm in your grasp.
Weaving with scarlet
Threads that are binding
Life strands entwining
Round Eternal path.

DECISIVENESS

DEBORAH

©1988 · L·LYNDE, C·ROSE

DEBORAH

Your prophecy piercing
Your judgement oft stinging
Accepting your own role,
Your importance as well.
A woman decisive
Yet open to nuance,
Aware of the great part
Others also must play.
Your political vision
Sees all tribes united,
As you sing the chorus
To victory's song.

GLEANING

© 1988. L·LYNDE, C·ROSE

RUTH

RUTH

Trusting your Mother
As you journey to her home
Joining the nation
You've chosen as your own.
Gleaning their rich fields
From corners as decreed
Filling your apron
With forgotten sheaves.
Lying on threshing floor
Beneath SHEKINAH'S wings
Healing ancestral wounds
Refreshing ancient springs.
Harvesting redeemers
From lines long entwined
Birthing a future
Divinely aligned.

INNER PRAYER

©1988 . L·LYNDE . C·ROSE

HANNAH

HANNAH

You pray "may my womb be open
Like my heart" and you're heard
Though, at first, not fully inderstood.
You're blessed with fruit,
Ripe and round,
Which you birth and rear
Until it is time again
To offer your essence
Upon the alter of love.

TIMING

ABIGAIL

©1993 L·LYNDE
C·ROSE

ABIGAIL

Young men called you shrewd.
They thought you comely, wise.
In haste, you bundled grain, set
loaves upon the asses and wine
to sweeten the decree of one
so wild, so full of rage he lost
all sight of the future. You
counselled him, calmed him,
helped him rise above his anger.
In time your vision came to pass.
David, King of Israel, and you
rightfully at his side.

WISDOM

© 1988 · L·LYNDE, C·ROSE

HULDAH

Huldah

Kings sought your wisdom
When wresting from chambers
Scrolls hidden mosslike
'Neath layers of stone.
While in the courtyard
Fragrant with jasmine
Sages sat learning
Laws from your tome,
Prophesis uttered
At gate of entry
Leaving a doorway
By your name known.

LEADERSHIP

ESTHER

ESTHER

Rather than remaining
Beauty queen chosen
You take up your own crown
And leadership claim.
Rather than playing the
Monarch's beloved
You take up your own crown
And bring about change.
Rather than revelling in
Status that's set apart
You take up your own crown
And admit your faith.
Rather than hiding your
Role in Divine scheme
You take up your own crown
And unmask your face.
Rather than disclaiming
Courageous strategy
You take up you own crown
And record the tale.

INTEGRITY

©1988. L·LYNDE, G·ROSE

JUDITH

JUDITH

With integrity
Judith, you act
In sync with the rhythms
Of your inner guide.
As though propelled by
A dream greater than
The human desire for
"Power over," you move
Into the centre of
The tent of life and death
And meet the challenge
That the moment presents.
This is the strength then
Your people celebrate
The victory of a woman
Who chooses her own fate.

CELEBRATION

© 1987 L·LYNDE
C·ROSE

MIRIAM

Biblical References

EVE: Genesis 2 and 3.

SARAH: Genesis 11:29-31; 12:5-17; 16:1-8; 17:15-21; 18; 20:2-18; 21:1-12; 23:1-19; 24:36, 37; 25:10, 12; 49:31; Isaiah 51:2.

REBEKAH: Genesis 22:23; 24; 25:20-28; 26:6-35; 27; 28:5; 29:12; 35:8; 49:31.

LEAH: Genesis 29; 30; 49:31; Ruth 4:11.

RACHEL: Genesis 29; 30; 31; 33:1, 2, 7; 35:16-26; 46:19, 22, 25; 48:7; Ruth 4:11; 1 Samuel 10:2; Jeremiah 31:15.

TAMAR: Genesis 38.

DINAH: Genesis 34.

MIRIAM: Exodus 2:1-10; 15:20-21; Numbers 12; 20:1; Micah 6:4.

TZIPPORAH: Exodus 2:16-22; 4:18-26; 18:1-7.

TRUST

RUTH

©1988, L. LYNDE GROSE

TZELOPHCHAD'S DAUGHTERS: Numbers 26:29-34; 27:1-11; 36; Joshua 17:3-6.

RAHAV: Joshua 2; 6.

DEBORAH: Judges 4, 5 .

RUTH: The Book of Ruth.

HANNAH: 1 Samuel 1, 2:1-21.

ABIGAIL: 1 Samuel 25.

HULDAH: 2 Kings 22:13-20; 2 Chronicles 34:22-28.

ESTHER: The Book of Esther.

JUDITH: The Book of Judith (The Apocrypha).

CAROL ROSE was awarded the National Canadian Jewish Book Award for Poetry for her first collection of poems, Behind the Blue Gate (1997), and has recently published a second collection, From the Dream (2013). She is co-editor of the anthology, Spider Woman: A Tapestry of Creativity and Healing (1999). She has toured widely with Mennonite poet Di Brandt performing their dialogical work Occupied Territories: An Argument in Poetry. Carol and husband, Rabbi Dr. Neal Rose, were honored in Winnipeg in January 2015 with the Lieutenant Governor's Award for the Advancement of Interreligious Understanding from the Province of Manitoba. Information about her workshops can be obtained from rose@ms.umanitoba.ca or mscarolrose.blogspot.com

9780692409138